The Only Way Out

Copyright © 2017 by Ahmad Rashad Perry Sr.

All rights reserved. No part of this book may be reproduced or transmitted in any form or by any means without written permission from the author.

Dedication

This book is dedicated to the most important people in my life. To my motherwhogavemeachanceatlife. You aremyangel, and Icannever repayyou. Thankyouforadopting me & saving my life and for always telling me the truth.

To my loving children Ahmadria, Sydney, Ahmad II. Your presence on Earth is divine. Neverlet anyone tell you anything different.

Table of Contents

Preface

Life is a process that is designed as a journey that involves continuous, internal, deliberate development. Many people negate the most important element which is ***trusting*** *process.* We fall into programmed -socialized facades and totally repudiate living life on our own terms.

You have decided to invest in yourself by purchasing this book, you must take accountability. Currently, you are being lead towards the direction of intentional growth. When you find changes all around you and in every area of your life, this shift of change means your *season* is changing.

The process of life involves season changes. Seasons change to create a cycle of growth. Spring doesn't skip to Fall, and Fall doesn't jump to Summer. If you can perceive this concept and apply it to your life, your journey will be so much more manageable. Consciously, we have to align our life with progression.

The process of life demonstrates that we are constantly entering a different season or a new place in life. The remarkable coincidence is that each season represents different types of challenges.

Winter

Winter is always ice cold. There are no leaves on the trees. The grass is brown and everything that once was, is gone. No matter how much you try to keep warm, it's cold the during the entire winter months. During winter, some animals hibernate. The Winter season is the time to process and plan. In your winter season, everything appears dormant and it may appear regardless to no matter how hard you, try nothing is getting accomplished. Winter is not for accomplishing, but for planning and processing new visions, hopes, connections, etc. Your winter season is when you should establish and gather the fuel (knowledge) that will generate your momentum and success.

Spring

We all know that when you cut all of your hair and it begins to grow back, there is an awkward stage that it goes through. Your hair will grow and will continue to grow and when it fully grows in its entirety, it's will be beautiful. It's sort of the same process when there is a transition from winter to spring. Spring is the beginning of nature's beauty and the season of provisions. In Spring, many new opportunities will emerge. The seeds of fall and the planning of winter will begin to bud & blossom. The season of Spring will bring many gloomy days because it is a rainy season. Nature looks bright and vibrant during the Spring, however, at the end of the season,everything will *seem* to wither, like everything is going wrong, when actually it's growing perfectly right. That rough patch that you will (and must) experience during this season is actually a sure indication that you are transitioning into a fruitful season. It's always cool, windy, and rainy at the beginning of Spring. At the end of this season, it's absolutely beautiful, definitely warm, the trees have all of their leaves, and the grass constantly grows.

Summer

As soon as it's hot outside, everybody is happy and ready to take the layers of clothes off that they were wearing the entire winter and some of spring. The belly rings are seen and the tramp stamps (lower back tatoos) are uncovered. Summer is your harvest season. It's the season that all the seeds that have been planted begin to harvest/manifest. The fruit of your labor will begin to appear. Summer is a season of intensity. Have you ever wondered why so many people are shot or why so many fights happen during the summer? It's because everything begins to heat up and the pressure increases because everything begins to move and grow at a rapid pace. Summer is a true season of testing. You have to make a decision to either pick all of your fruit because there is an abundance of them and they are ripe? Do you sell them or do you store for the Fall and Winter because eventually the Fall and Winter is right around the corner? The heat of the summer will either destroy the fruits of your labor or conjure a harvest beyond your imagination.

Fall

The Fall season is just as beautiful as the Spring and Summer. Please do not let the beautiful auburn and burnt orange colors fool you. Fall is the season that demonstrates that no matter how hard you try, nothing seems to go right. During your Fall Season, things just continue to fall apart. Instead of gaining, you begin to lose. You shed heavily. As the Fall season progress, the leaves on all of the trees all fall to the ground. Fall is a season when old blessings fall from your branches and new seeds are planted into the soils of your soul. With your changes during Fall, develops new hope, new convictions, new friends, just about everything is being created, recreated or rebirthed. Fall is the season for renewal. Ask yourself, what season are you currently experiencing?

Our perspective about everything that has occurred so far determines an outcome. Meaning, where you are currently in the growth process resembles the choices you have made. Whether it is *winter, spring, summer or fall*, you have created the circumstances that your life is enduring. *The Only Way Out* was written to help you prepare and thrive in all four seasons.

If there are dramatic positive changes happening, this is a result of the time you took to discipline your emotions. It is a manifestation of your commitment to intentional – purposeful - spiritual growth. If you are in the same place, the same circumstances, and the same situation, it is a result of your inability to commit to discipline. Believe it or not, the relationship you have with yourself and others, is the element used to exercise discipline. Chapter three-Toxic Relationships emphasizes how to deal with yourself and your intimate relationships. When you are conscious and aware of your reaction to life and people, you are committing yourself to intentional growth.

Growth is a process and it demands change. Physical change is something that happens no matter what. If you work out you will lose weight and have a pretty lean body. If you don't workout, let's just say you will not be in good physical shape. Intentional growth is being intentional regarding your growth which requires time, commitment, and discipline.

This book is segmented into chapters that represent purposeful growth. At different times in my life, I now realize, I was experiencing one of the four seasons in some way. Hindsight is always 20/20 but I wasn't equipped to manage certain circumstances or relationships because I wasn't intentional.

Introduction

Many of you who read this book have had the greatest blessing of all; being born in the United States of America. Although this is true, you hear stories of people living lives that they hate. Depression is at an all-time high, lives are unfulfilled, and there are more people who are miserable in the greatest land in the entire world than anywhere else. The NIMH stated, "In the United States, 16 million adults had at least one major depressive episode in 2012. That's 6.9 percent of the population. According to the World Health Organization (WHO), 350 million people worldwide suffer from **depression**. It is a leading cause of disability." How is this possible during the greatest time in human history?

The Only Way Out is your personal blueprint to escaping those unfulfilled emotions that reluctantly keep humans living a mundane life where their primary focus is paying bills & making ends meet. Whether you're interested in traveling more, taking more nature hikes, shopping, playing golf, or relaxing on the beach in Mexico, this is the treasure map that will assist you in achieving more of the things that will bring more fulfillment into your life; ultimately, changing your life forever.

You can escape poverty. Not only the environment, but the mindset as well. You can live the life of your dreams, and you can have total happiness and bliss because this is The Only Way Out. Anything less than living your ultimate life does humanity a disservice. First of all, you are not being humble. Secondly, you are not flying below the radar. Finally, you are causing a worldwide shortage of love and resources because you have not produced at your highest capacity.

The world needs more people who are in strong financial positions to help carry out the mission of eliminating poverty & ending wars. There's a small percentage of the population that control the world's wealth. Statistics suggest that more than two-fifths of the world's millionaires live in the US, followed by Japan with 7% and the UK with 6%." This select group of people make the rules, leaving the rest of us scrambling and disagreeing with the outcome as wellas the process. The chart below demonstrates this opinion.

Americans' debt

U.S. debt-to-income ratio by age group

Source: Credit Suisse Global Wealth Report, 2017

There's only one way to start the transition of getting out of this type of situation. This transition will not be easy, but it requires the general-public to work more as a community, rather than individuals.

Imagine twelve to twenty-four months from now, you're about to board a plane going to a tropical destination, a ski resort, or time away in solitude because you like to get in touch with nature. Whatever the ultimate life is for you, you're living it to the capacity which you're able to in as little as twenty-four months.

This journey of transitioning, there isn't a cookie cutter one size fits all approach. Each and every persons' life is different. The process will not all be the same but the fulfillment from this journey will feel the same with everyone that you meet onthis path. As an avid reader, *The Celestine Prophesy* by James Redfield suggest that, "for half a century now, a new consciousness has been entering the human world, a new awareness that can only be called transcendent, spiritual." James Redfield stated, "We begin to notice that chance events occur at just the right moment, and bring forth just the right individuals, to suddenly send our lives in a new and important direction. Perhaps more than any other people in any other time, we intuit higher meaning in these happenings."

Living the life of your dreams does not mean you must have a million dollars in the bank. If you're able to do what you want to do when you want to do it, to the capacity that you'd like to do it in, then you're living the life of your dreams. There will be some false starts and setbacks. There will be people who you thought should be encouraging, but you learned that they discouraged you at every turn. This is normal and considered par for the course. Let this be your reminder that you should keep going no matter what because this is The Only Way Out.

Chapter One

Erroneous Benchmarks

How is it that some people are born into loving caring families where the mother is a successful lawyer and father a doctor, but others are born to the mother of a heroin addict who dies before the kid could ever meet their parents? Why is that we are programmed into thinking the American dream is to attend college, marry, buy a house, have children, and then in-turn train our kids to follow the same path to become *accomplished?* Why is the divorce rate so high in America? Statistics suggest forty-one percent of first marriages end in divorce, sixty percent of **second** marriages end in divorce and seventy-three percent of **third** marriages end in divorce. But let's digress and start from the beginning –that is the beginning of life.

Being born is one of the single most phenomenal events known to mankind. Since being born is a phenomenal event, maybe that's why it's one of the most celebrated life events. People from every continent, no matter their cultural background or linguistic differences all celebrate the wonderful gift of life. This single thread ties the entire world together. We're all walking, breathing, living phonons.

Upon our arrival of birth to this strange land, is a grand mystery that we often don't contemplate, due to the daily hustle and bustle of life. However, if we, but for one moment dare try and wrap our minds around the fact that we're the results of roughly one in two hundred million, and this prodigious event has a certain magical element attached to it. That element provokes us to pursue the greater in life.

We come into this world without the ability to predetermine our circumstances. No one gets to choose the year, date, ethnicity, or financial circumstances they're born. With so many variables that exist beyond our control and the inexplicable flaws in the human psyche; it is impossible to be born without facing erroneous benchmarks.

Remember that child whose mother was a prostitute and heroin addict? Well her addiction forced her to leave her baby in a dumpster at four or five months. This child was me. I was placed in the system but fortunately adopted at eight months. My classmates or cousins didn't know that I was adopted. The bigger question is who could possibly do this to an innocent human being? Think about that for a second… There are only two reasons I know my mother is not my biological mother:

1) Her name is not on my original birth certificate, and 2) when I was three years old after getting in trouble for doing something, probably had no business doing, she tried to tell me. This unforgettable memory has molded my character and created the relentless individual I am today. Imagine thinking that the person you knew as *mom* was not your mother. It's an unfathomable thought but because of the love she selflessly gave me then and now, I am able to speak openly and pen this book about how these circumstances designed my life's path.

As a child, we're not aware of our socio-economic environment. How much money your family has is never a question; until you notice the bullying that you're taking at school because your school clothes does not meet the standards of the status quo. These years are critical for the development of your sense of self in a world that is constantly bombarding us with images of things we need to make our lives better. The memories of my childhood are filled with enjoyable moments. Some of my best memories as a child was running through the woods, climbing trees, and pretending to drive eighteen wheelers while riding a ten-speed mountain bike. That was childhood; the years where everything appeared out of osmosis.

I recall in middle and high school once we got home from school, we would go right into eating everything because it was there, not because we were hungry. My mother would usually say something funny, but serious like, "Stop eating all of the food! I just bought it." In my feeble mind, I had no clue why she constantly would repeat that phrase over and over and over again, after shopping for food. However, the underlining statement of why my mother would repeat that phrase over-and-over again was a statement directly tied to her awareness that the food needed to last for two weeks until she got paid again. At the rate we were eating, she would be back in the grocery store within the week, in between paychecks, and short of cash to buy even more food.

As a kid, I wasn't aware that we were poor. Not having cable or enjoying the luxuries of a computer like a kid who grew up to a white-collared family of workers was just not customary. Being poor was not a thought until I was eleven. We had no running hot water and to bathe, I would fill eight one-gallon jugs from outside, boil the water so that it was hot and then stand in front of the stove and bathe in a foot tub from the hospital.

Where was my dad during all of this? My biological dad was in Michigan and was not present in my life. He worked as a construction worker. Although he married my mom, they divorced when I was four. Fast forward to age twenty-eight; in 2012, my father died of congestive heart failure, but our relationship was estranged. Of course, there were male role models (uncles, coaches, etc.) in my life, but I was angry because I wanted a relationship with my father.

Receiving the new Jordan sneakers were so far away from my reality that I quickly began to become secure within myself as an individual. Security was within me, not because of the clothes that I wore, but because of the person that I was. I had a deeper sense of self, due to the pain that I lived with up until this point and time of my life. In time, as we grow and develop on this earth, we come to realize that it's the intangible things that shape, influence and form our world more than anything else. For example, nothing we can see or touch can come into existence without the precious force of thought. Our thoughts and imaginations produce every physical thing we encounter. Rhonda Byrne influenced the world with *The Secret* which is the viewpoint and belief of focused thoughts (positive or negative) creating experiences. Our *thoughts* about "something" is what determines its significance in our society.

Who determines which has greater value: silver or gold?

Or who determines what should cost more: water or oil? The answer is we do. Through our ever shifting, growing, and developing thought process we determine what is or should be considered of great value. The intangible force of thought can be transferred to other people and shapes the world in which we live.

The unavoidable flaw in this part of our existence is how subjective our thoughts are about things. In a world with a population of roughly 7.5 billion people on seven different continents, standards are subject to change. Having the change in standards, leaves us all at the mercy of benchmarks or standards that can be deemed erroneous. Understanding and embracing, the change in standards, can infuse and propel us on our journey as we navigate through life. My world was never the same once I found out I was adopted. Daily, it wasas if I knew something that no one else did. I was a secret kid. The secret guy that got the attention from other family members. I was the teacher's pet. I was the kid in church who everyone hugged and looked at with a little more compassion & empathy. I was special because of my secret & painful existence.

Although our family environment was filled with love, joy, and a bunch of laughter, I knew there was something slightly off. After my mother informed me of my adoption, my sensitivity was extremely high. I was usually the teacher's pet, but if she called my name too loud, I would cry. My aunts would immediately kiss or give me the biggest hug when they saw me and I loved every minute of the "over-attention" I received.

But there was a void within that I could never fill and barely understood. I could be in the midst of a family gathering (we have a pretty big family), but I would feel alone. I would feel left out and as I type this section of the book, I'm with a portion of my family in the cabins in Tennessee, but I still feel alone. I was the child that was different. Now, as an adult - that's different, this feeling will probably never go away.

Through our subjective and sub-conscious minds, we all live by the general consensus of the majority rules. Once the *majority* place value on a particular thing, it's settled.

Professor Micheal Munger believes, "Majority rules is a way of choosing. Democracy is a system that ensures government is responsible for the majority and the individual. The problem when we choose majority rules is that the majority may want to decide everything, not just the issues in the proper domains set out in the constitution."

So, upon our entrance into this world, many benchmarks have already been etched. People who are born in the same general area may not even know that these benchmarks even exist. I didn't know they existed until years after I left my hometown. I realized the level of academic potential that I possessed as a student was not applied.

I realized the potential I possessed during the Marine Corps basic training and the opportunity to utilize this new mindset and confidence was set before me daily. I often began to wonder about the things I could have accomplished if I only applied this confidence at earlier times in my teenage life.

In certain environments, different things are valued. For example, diamonds are valuable. Those who possess them will have access to a great life on earth; it appears. Although these precious stones have no practical use beyond a drill bit, we deem them valuable therefore they are.

If you're born in a society that is lacking access or control of certain resources you are considered "poor." This condition can be altered based on your ability to obtain whatever your society considers valuable at the time in which you are born. This book isn't written to alter the philosophy of what a society considers valuable. It is written for the people in this generation and at this time of human existence to be empowered to obtain financial freedom.

This section of the book is given to unify you with inner tenacity to overcome any errors beyond your control that may prevent you from living out your dreams. By simply building a case through logical reasoning that we're all faced with circumstances beyond our control. However, we don't have to allow any set of predetermined circumstances to control our destinies while we are here.

Escaping erroneous standards and mentalities is key if we ever want to live out our dreams. Many of us come from communities or homes that have had little or no concept of what the benchmarks of wealth are in society. I know speaking from personal experience here in America that a consumers' mentality was very prevalent in my community. Which leads automatically equating self-worth with the things I could purchase. This benchmark is contagious and erroneous. This thought process has and will continue to lead many of us down a barren path of misappropriation ofresources.

I remember my first mentor; a real estate investor. He equipped me with the knowledge to obtain my first property at the age of twenty. After purchasing my first home, there wasn't much you could tell me about life. I thought I knew it all. I thought Ihad all the answers. My peers came to me and asked questions about everything. I noticed that the appearance of success creates a false perception of general knowledge. I sold that house twelve months later and made more money than I had ever seen in one lump sum at that time in my life. Again, no one could tell me anything at the time. Three months later, those resources were completely depleted.

As stated earlier, being born in an upper-class family can bring erroneous benchmarks as well. The child born, whose parents who could be a high-level corporate executive or a physician can live with the pressures of trying to out-perform their parent's levels of success. However, data proves that most of these kids live in the shadows of their parents. This could lead to large amounts of pressure on the individual if they are pursuing something that they have no interest in doing.

Beyond misappropriating resources is the deteriorating side effects of low self-esteem and self-worth. Many people still find themselves being haunted with these side effects long after they've escaped their environments. Although their financial status has changed, the way they view money and the way they view themselves has not.

It's imperative that we liberate ourselves from on-going thoughts of hopelessness. These behavioral patterns lead to financially and emotionally destructive habits. Correcting how we address these inaccurate benchmarks are not just another path or approach to life, it's our only way out.

It is expected for children who grow up on the lower end of the socioeconomic spectrum to have very little accomplishments in life. Research is showing that children on the other end of this scale have problems as well. These families appear to have it all. The houses are nice, the communities are nice, and their children are attending private schools. On the other hand, some of these children have emotional problems, such as, eating disorders, and many other behavioral issues that are destructive that allows them to deal with the stress ofperformance.

Madeline Levine, psychiatrist and author of *The Price of Privilege* completed "numerous studies indicating that privileged adolescents are experiencing epidemic rates of depression, anxiety disorders, and substance abuse--rates that are higher than those of any other socioeconomic group of young people in this country. The various elements of a perfect storm--materialism, pressure to achieve, perfectionism, disconnection--are combining to create a crisis in America's culture of affluence. This culture is as unmanageable for parents--mothers in particular--as it is for their children. While many privileged kids project confidence and know how to make a good impression, alarming numbers lack the basic foundation of psychological development: an authentic sense of self. Even parents often miss the signs of significant emotional problems in their "star" children."

The pressures of performance on individuals from well to do backgrounds can have the same exploding impact as the pressure of escaping poverty. The anxiety is detrimental on both sides. I have provided are two different examples of children being in circumstances with anxiety being the common denominator.

Chapter Two

Dream Killers

There is nothing more precious or enjoyable as the limitless imaginations of a child. Upon our entry into this world, we are all equipped with the greatest creative force known to man; possessing a living, breathing, life-giving imagination. We can all attest that there has not been a greater contribution to humanity apart from our treasure filled imaginations.

I am sure from time to time we find ourselves dreaming or fantasizing about the possibilities of a different and more enjoyable tomorrow. In these moments, we're operating at our highest level of creative thinking. We're exploring the possibilities of life in our hearts. These places that we enter are the places where dreams are born and lives are altered forever.

Can you imagine the excitement and adrenaline that was pulsating through Orville and Wilbur as they dreamed of a machine that could soar with the eagles? Picture in your mind, there they were, in a bicycle shop in Dayton, Ohio dreaming of flying. It is hard to imagine a world without airplanes. Can you believe that it was just a little over a century ago, the thought of flying seemed far-fetched and simply impossible? Guess what, so is the power of the human imagination and the courageousness of adreamer.

The primary key to living out a dream is the ability to hold on to the joy and excitement we first experienced when we first dreamt of doing what our eyes thought was impossible. Our lives have benefited a great deal because of dreamers. Along with those who allowed their passion and excitement to lead them down the winding path of possibilities. Just imagine, where would we be if Martin Cooper hadn't allowed that excitement and passion to lead him to construct the first cell phone.

Our dreams give birth to endless possibilities and inspiration for all those who dare to live beyond what they can see. Having the audacity to dream is the single most significant quality that we carry with us daily. Although, we all carry this quality with us to some degree, our greatest capacity to dream was when we were children. Then, every single creative thought seemed possible! Somehow life has short circuited our creative juices because of all of its logic, reasoning, and rationale.

As we grow older, many of our creative abilities start to diminish unintentionally. We have exchanged our child-like excitement for more "reasonable" patterns of thinking. Along with many of our peers, we find ourselves being more acquainted with our limitations than our possibilities.

Somewhere between childhood and adulthood we allowed our dreams to die slowly.

At the young age of eighteen, two days after graduating high school, I joined the Marines. One of my goals or desires was to attend the University of Alabama, but I didn't get the basketball scholarship I was striving for, so I decided to join the military. Remember, I grew up poor. Deep down, I knew it was my responsibility to change that stigma for my family. I also didn't want to go to college and get stuck in a small country town that was not industrialized. Living in a much bigger city was the ultimate goal. After speaking with the recruiters and was sold on the dream or idea that the military could pay for me to go to college, I decided this would be a win-win situation. Making that decision helped me to recognize that my life was partially controlled byDream Killers.

Why was the decision *I* made to enroll in the military seen as detrimental? Why didn't my family see that this was a great opportunity for me to mature? What is so ironic is Dream Killers don't even realize that they are Dream Killers. Unintentionally, they do not recognize there are more possibilities outside their experiences, habits and conditions. What was seen as the wrong decision for me, through everybody else's eye, was one of the best choices I made for my future.

Remember when you are progressive, you automatically experience resistance. It is so imperative to align yourselfwith others who have the same mindset. You should never allow your vision to die because of the negativity or ignorance of others.

Life is all about the details. At this point in my life, I had to learn and relearn some behaviors. By becoming a Marine, I learned structure and the importance of details. A Marine is very meticulous because details matter. Here, I was taught there are no limitations to what you can do if you push through the pain. Pain is weakness leaving the body and mind. Being in the Marine Corp., made me feel like I could do anything. Nothing would stop me especially once I'd set my mind to do it. If I set my mind to lose forty pounds I could do it. If I wanted to run three miles in under eighteen minutes, I could do it if I pushed myself. This is the point in my life, where I learned that I wouldn't die if I pushed myself to the limits. From that moment forward, I started believing in myself more.

Being a soldier in the Marine Corp., I learned true comradery. On the battlefield - you never leave a fallen soldier. Here is where I learned to build friendships with men who were considered my brothers and we were to never leave a brother behind. The Marine Corp taught me that most individuals are naturally weak. Here is where I learned that I got more done before 6am than what most people get done in a day. Joining the Marine taught me that there are only a few good men.

When I was twenty years old most of my peers were still in college. This is when I purchased my first home. The real estate investor I spoke briefly about in chapter one took me under his wing and began mentoring me about everything; real estate and life. Meeting him changed my perception of entrepreneurship and how the rich conductedthemselves. First of all, I didn't know that he was rich based off of his appearance, as well as, the fact that he showed up to work every day. We perceive rich people as those who do not work, have no problems and spend all of their time enjoying the luxuries of an overelaborated lifestyle.

Retired from the Air force, my mentor built a real estate empire and still worked a nine to five as a government employee. He taught me about trading stocks. When he finally revealed that he owned an apartment complex my mind was shattered. How was someone able to own an apartment complex, make three million dollars per year off of that complex and be employed with the government as a nine to five employee?

This experience immediately taught me to believe in having multiple streams of income and negated the idea that the wealthy people do not work. Most are led to believe that you must have five or more streams of income to be wealthy. I believe that is a very misleading idea. As the mentee to two millionaires, which stream of income are two extremely successful businesses, this theory leads me to that conclusion.

CNBC.com has written an article by Katie Little entitled *Ten Traits Rich People Have In Common.* The ten traits support the ultimate idea of intentional growth and living the life of your dreams.

Ten Traits The Opulent Have In Common

1. They built wealth for the long haul: Most of their sizable accounts came from earned income andinvesting.

2. They've nailed the basics: This group didn't realize their biggest wins by taking big risks. Instead, 86 percent said the biggest gains came through buying and holding investments while 89 percent attributed their biggest wins to traditional stocks and bonds.

3. They're optimistic (and opportunistic): The group's opinion on investment return potential over the next year skews more optimistic than pessimistic, and they're ready to invest when they see an opportunity. One in five surveyed kept more than 25 percent of their assets in cash, in large part to pouncewhen they see buying opportunities.

4. They use credit strategically: Nearly two in three use credit to build their wealth.

5. They keep a close eye on the Tax Man: They are very attuned to potential tax implications of their decisions, with 55percent saying investment moves that factor these in are better to pursue than high returns.

6. They diversify in valuable tangible assets: Almost half invest in these assets, including timber properties, investment real estate and farmland. About 20 percent collect fine art.

7. They're disciplined: About four out of five surveyed said investing to meet long-term goals is more important than making money for short-term wants andneeds.

8. They had strong examples growing up: While the wealthy do not typically come from wealthy backgrounds, the majority were raised by parents who encouraged them to pursue their interests but set firm boundaries. About four out of five said this was true about their childhood. These five values were stressed more while the wealthy were growing up: "academic achievement, financial discipline, work participation, family loyalty and civic duty."

9. They love giving back: About two-thirds said their family had a strong tradition of philanthropy.

10. They're committed at home: This group is far from single and ready to mingle. A full 86 percent of the HNW investors surveyed are married or in long-term relationships.

I kept hanging around him and my beliefs began to change. The saying, if you hang around nine millionaires, you will become the tenth became my mantra. Receiving awards for maintaining the various military standards, seemed like the blessings that I deserved because of the pain and circumstances of my childhood. Everything I thought I knew about life, I began to challenge and started retraining my brain at twenty.

Was it a bad idea to join the Marine Corps? Why and how did my family get stuck in the mindset of poverty and lack?

Growing up, my family was Baptist and very religious. Although my faith was strong, during this period of success, I questioned and challenged topics, especially about money. Emotionally, I began to believe I was pushing for too much. Like maybe my goals were too lofty? Or maybe I took myself too seriously?

People do not have the capacity to believe in the *unbelievable* based off of their circumstances. Memories of guilt started to form subconsciously. Most of my family never came to visit the house that I purchased. I often wondered what their reason for never coming to visit. Anyone will be frustrated in a situation of finding out that most dream killers are people that you hold in high regards, or that it is the people that you care about the most.

I remember wanting to rent out some of our heirs property and presented the idea to a couple family members - they totally ignored the concept and the idea of making this a reality. Back then, I didn't force the idea. With my limited knowledge and only two years of new any found discoveries, I couldn't challenge them. Besides they were older and knew what they were talking about. Right? They were older and had experienced life. My idea of success was what they were doing. I didn't realize that the information that I was presenting was a new concept totally dissimilar of what they were accustomed too.

Dream Killers don't realize they are killing dreams. They believe they are giving their opinion. One reason, I don't like giving my opinion is because opinions are irrelevant. My opinion about your life and what you are doing carries no weight. We are sometimes paralyzed by the opinion from others.

You have to fight for your ability to create. Stand on your idea of self instead of what everybody else wants you to be.

At all times, no matter what your age, believe in yourself and fight for your ideas. If you are talking to someone about an idea, two things are going to happen; (1) either they won't understand because they don't have enough information to understand what you want to do, or (2) they won't care.

Dream killers have limitations on their mind. Their earning potential is capitalized and limited by their thoughts. We all know there are risks involved with this optimistic way of thinking. We take risk every single day, even though, we have been conditioned to fear taking risk. Taking risks is the only way to financial freedom. Independence is simply living and becoming the person you were created and destined to be.

People respond to others who have massive success. They have an ego or an edge to perform at a higher level. Your ego makes you chase the vision in your mind and keeps you in check. Maybe my family didn't come to visit because I was ego-tripping. I guess I will never know but I do knowthatyou do need your ego. You should only use it when you need itswisdom.

From my limited perspective, the ego is a driving force within each of us that keeps thriving to achieve more. You may have everything you need but in the back of your mind there's a small voice that says, MORE. That's ego. There's nothing wrong with striving to do and have more for the greater good of the community, but if this is mixed with arrogance, thelack of self-control, or the disregard for another human being, then that is when huge problems arise. Shortly after, this point in my life, I failed miserably. Life humbled me while teaching me to tame my ego. Failure will teach you this each time.

Every decision you make brings a dream killer. The question is are you going to press beyond the resistance? You cannot be negatively impacted by a blow. Realize you must take blows to be promoted. You have to push through…I've come to realize that life is filled with dream killers. Some are more subtlethan others. Life is like a field of land mines riddled with snares, traps, and pitfalls that kill dreams. Once a dream dies, a place in the dreamer's heart dies as well.

The death of a dreamer's heart is one of the saddest truths I've encountered in my short lifetime on this earth. The purpose of this segment is to identify some of those land mines in hopes of avoiding them. My highest desire is to reawaken you to dream again, to believe again, and to resurrect a dream that may have died long ago.

Here is the part that will be hard for some of you to stomach. Talking about living the life of your dreams is exciting. The thought of pain being associated with who you are becoming brings up another issue. There is something deep down within that has been craving to emerge. Your responsibility is to find a way to carve off the excess layers around your superior self. Think for a moment about how a child is brought into this world. The sperm is planted into the egg. It begins to grow over forty weeks. The woman's body goes through changes that are uncomfortable. These changes are noticeable to anyone in her presence. Her walk changes. Her nose may spread. Her sense of smell is heightened. Some foods may make her sick. These things are happening as a human being is growing within her body.

During that tenth month, she goes into labor and gives birth to a child if she was fortunate enough to carry for the entire pregnancy. She is faced with death during child labor. Once she holds that child, she forgets the pain for a brief second because she is holding the miracle of life in her hands.

My point in bringing this imagery to mind is to correlate the painful process of childbirth. *Birthing* the life of your dreams will be no different. It may take weeks, months, or even years for some ideas to evolve into full fruition. Continue with the ideas until they take on a life of its own. You will go through numerous changes. You will notice changes in your mental process and your environment. You may notice that you are associating with people you normally don't deal with. You may also notice that these people will push you and hold you accountable in reaching your goals.

Understanding that pain is a part of the process and becoming greater deters many people away from doing more. No one wants to purposefully put themselves through uncomfortable circumstances. We like comfort and complacency. We must understand that comfort is the enemy of growth and success. Comfort is the reason many don't ever realize their ultimate potential. You have a superhero inside of you, but you're sitting on the couch watching the television. Get up and start doing the necessary work to make your ideas tangible and a reality.

No one is above the need for encouragement. Neither is anyone above the overwhelming darkness that can invade one's life in the face of harsh cruel criticism. From the moment we take our first step until we begin to run and leap for the stars, our natural response to words are indescribable. Have you ever seen the way a child responds to the affirming words of a parent? It's amazing how the vibrations from our voice ca n provoke them to fits of excitement and titillation.

UNAUTHORIZED VOICES

We learn very early in life what deserves an applaud. I have a friend that always says, "I'll clap when I am impressed." These inarguable elementary truths have taught me a lot about life. It has taught me the power of the spoken word. As well as, its effects on how I view life. We live in a voice activated world and everyone we encounter are products of the things they've heard. Knowing this one simple truth gives us the ability to transform and reshape everything around us.

Once we accept the power of words and their ability to infuse and steer us in one way or another, we have valuable keys. These keys give us access to a world of possibilities. Acknowledging that this power has been given to everyone who has a voice is valuable information. Once we acknowledge this truth, we'll be sure to regulate the voices we allow to speak into our hearts.

We must acknowledge not everyone has jurisdiction to speak into our lives. So many dreams remain in a feeble state of existence. We see this occur simply because the dreamer allowed an unauthorized voice to speak to them. Everyone has power, but every voice doesn't have a place in our lives. These voices are the primary proponents of dreams deferred and unrealized. Listening to "unauthorized voices" and above all other land mines in our lives is chief among dream killers.

Acknowledging the truth regarding "unauthorized voices" requires a response. We must be willing to be misunderstood in most cases and even disliked in others. Simply because we can't allow any voice to alter or deter our destinies. Our dreams are treasures and must be guarded with our lives. Let us never forget our dreams harness the very destiny of our children. Along with every other valuable asset we have. We can't allow anything or anyone to damage it.

One of the most difficult things to do on our journeys is to sever ties with relatives whose words can potentially kill our dreams. I've seen cases where people would spend long periods of time away from friends and family just to give birth to their dream

Usually it's those closest to you who's the hardest to convince that your dream is an attainable reality. Most times we have to either remove ourselves from them in order to live out our dream, or never share it with them at all.

For a brief moment, I'd like you to make a short list of people who are close to you that are the most prone to being pessimistic. Now I want you to imagine your dream as a beautiful infant. Everyone who you just placed on your list has a virus. Think of any virus that can kill rapidly, something like Ebola or Marburg. Would you allow that person access to your baby? We have to use the same train of thought about our dreams.

We have to possess the same tenacity and vigor to protect our dreams as we do an innocent child. We must apply this very same logical train of thought as when we're protecting an innocent life. If you woke up in the morning and read a news feed about a parent who intentionally exposed their child to someone with a deadly virus, you'd call them insane.

In fact, most of us would be down-right livid with that person for being so reckless and irresponsible. Many of us would even go as far as saying, "Anyone who would do such a horrible thing should be locked up! How dare you take an innocent child and knowingly expose him/her to Ebola! Are you nuts?" When we all allow our dreams to fall into the hands of negative relatives and friends, we're doing the exact same thing.

We must transform our train of thought when it applies to how we view our dreams. We must assume the role of a loving parent nurturing a child. Once we do this, it becomes more apparent the severity of the responsibility we hold as guardians. The gravity of this responsibility makes it easier to ward off family and friends in our process of developing a child. Your dream is your child.

Chapter Three

Toxic Relationships

Toxic relationships have no respect of person. Think about all of the friendships, partnerships, and relationships that you are currently in. If that someone is constantly causing an extreme shift in your emotional well-being, it is a toxic relationship. Nothing or no one should be allowed to drastically change your reaction, mood, or temperament.

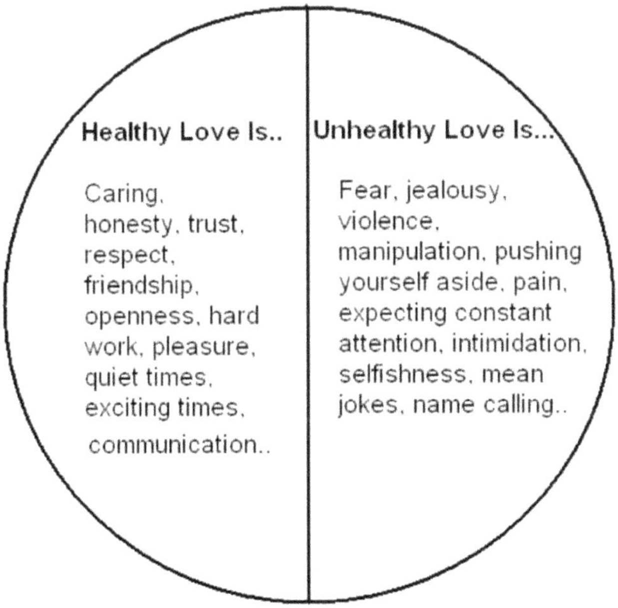

Healthy Love Is..	Unhealthy Love Is...
Caring, honesty, trust, respect, friendship, openness, hard work, pleasure, quiet times, exciting times, communication..	Fear, jealousy, violence, manipulation, pushing yourself aside, pain, expecting constant attention, intimidation, selfishness, mean jokes, name calling..

EQ or Emotional Intelligence is an ideology created by John Mayer and Peter Salovey. In the 90's, this philosophy became very popular and not only do companies utilize EQ to determine who would be a good fit for a particular job, it could be a great way to determine compatibility when dealing with any type of relationship. The only way out of *toxic relationships* is to understand mutual respect for another human beings and that it should be reciprocated.

Emotional stability single handedly is the driving force of relationships. Without any self-control or developed habits of mutual respect, toxic relationships will continue to exist. In order to successfully master what you bring to a relationship, managing your emotions should be the central focus.

According to Mayer, and Salovey, emotional intelligence has five segments:

I. Self-awareness- the ability to understand what drives our moods and emotions

II. Self-regulation – the ability to control our emotions and impulses

III. Internal motivation-inner strength that is developed through good habits and being an optimist

IV. Empathy-recognizing and understanding the emotions of others

V. Social Skills- being able to utilize some extroverted personality traits to co-exist with others

Toxic relationships occur because people are not effective communicators and are not aware of their emotional intelligence. Individuals who are very talkative by nature, sometimes, aren't really effective listeners.

Think about the many times you have been in a conversation with someone and the person heard what they wanted to hear because they were too busy trying to express their concern or point? How many times have you been in a relationship where expressions of perspective were misconstrued because the communication of thought or subject went left verses right? How could someone who has had several failed relationships give advice about toxic relationships? With ease. I know what causes a relationship to go south.

At the age of twenty-one, I was the father of two and now husband to a wife. My first child's mother lived in Alabama and we dated on and off my last two years of high school. We were pretty close nit and many people thought we were going to get married; however, I was unsure, and that uncertainty caused the relationship to turn toxic.

As I mentioned before, relationships can start off normal, but if expectations are not met; the relationship can turn toxic. It is up to you to determine if this type of relationship will be something that you will want to deal with every day ofyour life. All relationships will at some point challenge you to be better and that relationship has definitely done that for my life.

It is not normal to argue about every single detail of daily events. It is not normal to feel like you're living in a prison because who you really are as a person is not acceptable to who you are in a relationship with. These relationships could very well be the most detrimental threat to who you are becoming and what you are trying to build. No matter where I go or what I achieve I do not consider my accomplishments better than the tone of this first relationship. That first relationship keeps me humble because it reminds me of every mistake I've made, and I believe that it's a good thing.

The relationship with the mother of my first child was on the rocks when I left for Marine Corps boot camp. During my time away, we exchanged letters and stayed connected. However, I would hear rumors of her hanging out in the clubs. I didn't like the idea of my lady friend partying while I was away. At the time, I didn't realize that I had deep trust issues with women, and I didn't trust her.

Eventually, we split but not without her getting pregnant. She gave birth to my oldest daughter and I had to grow up quick. I was nineteen and I had no clue of what it meant to Father a child. However, I thought I was grown. There wasn't anything my elders could tell me. I was making my own money, I wasn't living at home, and I wasn't planning on moving back after I was done with my military duties. Not marrying her caused more pain and agony in my life than anything else. We argued all the time. Eventually, this led to me not talking to my daughter too much because I'd have to interact and speak with her mother. This day, our relationship is still toxic. We don't communicate. We don't co-parent. My relationship with my oldest daughter is estranged.

After being introduced to my first ex-wife by my Pastor at the time, I felt a strong obligation to marry her. This relationship started off normal as well, however in this relationship life's pressures made things toxic.

In 2004, I sold the house and made sixty thousand! Do you see the excitement I still possess fourteen years later because of that one accomplishment? It was surreal because I had never seen that much money at one time in my entire short-lived life. After completing four years in the Marine, my career choice led me into finance. Accepting the role of an Investment Advisor was another challenge, even though making $22,000 my first week in the role propelled my ego and my thought process.

How could a kid who grew up very poor in one of the smallest towns in Alabama make $82,000 in less that twelve months? Not understanding financial literacy caused me to spend $82,000 in two months. I thought I was rich. I remember telling my mother she no longer had work and the effect of that decision was her telling all of my family members. Everyone was asking for money and I didn't mind sharing because Iwas under the illusion I had more than enough.

Being able to send money to them to go to the casino or for them to do whatever made me feel like someone of high importance. I enjoyed this *god-like* feeling for only sixty days but experienced depression for four years afterwards. I became toxic.

From 2005 to 2009, I was depressed. I began searching and figured out a way to deal with this depression. I felt like a failure, but I had to feed my kids. I joined the Army to make sure that obligation was being met. Weekly, I read two to three books. I had to figure out how I allowed this money to literally slip through my fingers. Forced into a humbled state, I began reading books about money.

Ninety-eight percent of the population make money but only two percent possess knowledge on how to make it grow. The wealthiest is the two percent of society.

Lost jobs, certifications, and income equals pressure from the in-laws and that can cause a young relationship to go south very quickly. We have two beautiful-intelligent children and similar to the previous relationship, this relationship reminded me of how imperfect I was and still am.

Introspection can be also be referred to as self-awareness, is indispensable when dealing with others. Checking in with yourself to ensure that you are whole, and that respect is being represented in all of your interactions with others helps eliminate poison-toxins between relationships. This very day, I am humbled by my mistakes. I am also hopeful that the future will be better because of these mistakes made at a young age.

If success is the goal but escaping toxic situations is an objective, you have to be aware of the pain that is associated with the transition. Pain is a part of your journey. Shattering the beliefs that have limited your life will not be easy. This process does not happen over-night, unless you immerse yourself deeply into the transition.

For instance, it takes ninety days to see the results for a workout regimen. However, when people step into the gym to become healthier, they expect results immediately. We do thisin every area of our lives. We expect results immediately in a new business. We expect results immediately in investing. We expect results immediately in mostly everything we set out to do. No one wants to go through the painful process of transformation.

When building muscle, you are sore until your body gets comfortable with the new activity. Building your financial muscle works the same. It is a task to live in America and have the discipline to take risk with capital and to live below your means. We are socialized to spend money as soon as we get paid. For most of us, the thought of investing is painful. We run from that pain.

Putting your mind in painful circumstances will help you create critical thinking skills. It will help calm your nerves when you are uncomfortable. You won't panic over small things. You will be able to see problems and solve them quickly. You will be able to trust your genius.

On this journey, I have had several circumstances that were uncomfortable. What I realized is each new discomfort was an opportunity for me to sharpen my blade as a problem solver and a creator. I identify problems quickly and solve them. It was not always easy. Not being able to stay calm in every situation had a significant cost. I have lost valuable things along the way, but I did not stay in that defeated place. I kept going. Detach your emotions from critical moments. You will come out on top on the other end.

I currently use the painful moments in my life as fuel to keep getting better. It burns deeply to wake up in my house without my children. My idea of fatherhood was to have my children living under the same roof as myself. The realization of this dream not coming to reality burns like fire. The reminder is there daily. Although I feel this way when that thought crosses my mind, I remain positive and optimistic. The motivation that keeps me going is knowing that I have made mistakes. You have made mistakes. I try not to be too hard on myself and I am never too hard on others who have made mistakes as well. It's apart of the process and we are in control of how the story ends.

Most times when we hear the phrase toxic relationship, we immediately look to another person to blame. In intimate relationships, I was the common denominator. I had to dig deep within myself to determine what had gone wrong and why these relationships went south. You will never level up or be promoted into maturity and growth if you continuously overlook your mistakes.

Accountability is essential while evaluating your efforts to become better. I realized during my second divorce that I lackedemotional validation and emotional awareness. Although my IQ is very high my EQ was low, but balance must be maintained in every aspect of our lives.

Men are taught to be producers, to be strong, and to be the protectors of their families. In the old days most men would come home on Friday night (if he came home), grab a bottle of alcohol and drink for the entire weekend while sitting in a recliner. If you're laughing right now, you probably recall a male that you know doing that as you grewup.

In this day and age, it is required of men to be more emotionally aware of the impact that they're having in their households. In my marriages and the relationship with my first daughter's mother, I can pin-point the lack of validation, emotional stability, and the lack of emotional awareness. I've statedittwice – *I lacked emotional stability and emotional awareness in both marriages.*

The transition between my first ex-wife and second ex-wife included a few relationships in between but ended quickly. There were too many issues that made us incompatible.

I was chasing my dream of becoming an entrepreneur when my first marriage was coming to an end. We both knew that we were no longer compatible, but we had two children and we were trying to make it work.

As stated earlier, one of the most challenging moments of my life was leaving the home where my children were. How would I ever be the man that I wanted to be without living in the house with my children? I would never be able to get rid of the stigma of being divorced with three children. I was determined to not be categorized by stereotypes or statistics. Continuing a career in sales was not at all appealing to my first ex-wife. She considered sales more like a hobby because the pay wasn't guaranteed. Once the divorce was complete, I began to have success in my sales career. I was able to focus on my craft and build.

Making the decision to go back into the military while I rebuilt my inner strength and mindset allowed me to really understand that life is really short. Being sent on tour to Iraq provided me with the reality that I could die in any given moment. Everyone that loved me would live on. They would be sad, but they would live on…in that moment I realized I had the power to create my life and the vision that I saw in my head, I could manifest into reality.

There was a time when I thought that being abandoned was tragic. The thought and feeling of the person you love one day leaving, paralyzed me to the core. I created psychological and emotional barriers to protect myself from this type of trauma. If we are truthful with ourselves, the fear of losing thatperson, that job, the house, or the car is an emotion that paralyzes many of us.

There were several stages throughout my life where I came to grips with some of these emotions. Being deployed to Iraq forced me to face the facts. I attained freedom once I realized that we as humans could be here today and gone tomorrow. No longer would I make decisions based on the expectations of others.

Detaching your emotions from the expectations of others comes with a price. You will be ridiculed because you're not moved or bothered by their opinions. You will be judged when you hold the things you value without letting go. You will be called crazy, cold-hearted, and the name calling list goes on and on. Do not allow average opinions to knock you off of your path. You must go through to the end of this emotional journey. There is no other way of living the life of your dreams without being presented with challenges to overcome.

For the most part, you'll have to face these emotions alone. Yes, you will have friends around you offering up their best advice. Relatives will likely throw in their two cents as well. However, the ultimate choice will be left up to you. You are solely responsible. You cannot blame anyone else for not attaining the goals that you set for yourself. Will you push yourself through the weak areas of your life to become stronger? Only time will time.

Within the last six to nine months, I've experienced several moments that I've had to push through. I was weak in a lot of areas. Emotional stability and being validated by some of my accomplishments professionally, created an illusion that I couldn't be touched. Being caught in the middle of a second divorce, humbled me in some ways that I may not be able to write in this book. However, I learned that the fear of being abandoned was not so bad after all. Good things can come out of not so good situations.

There's a power that lies under the ashes. Each day dealing with the fact that my second ex-wife was no longer coming back, made me question certain areas of my life that I neglected on this journey. Not being emotionally aware in critical moments or responding too brash in situations was blamed on being focused on my vision. Unaware of what I was bringing to these intimate relationships, forced me into reflection. Now, I understand that I lacked the emotional validation needed to sustain.

Rest in the guarantee that your validation can only be found in a higher power. Something much bigger than yourself. The intelligence of life and of this universe. That's the powerful source of validation for myself and the person who's holding this book. Making this statement correlates with 2 Corinthians chapter four verses six and seven: "For God, who said, "Let light shine out of darkness," made his light shine in our hearts to give us the light of knowledge of God's glory displayed in the face of Christ. But we have this treasure in jars of clay to show that this all-surpassing power is from God and not from us."

There is a power working within our souls that brings validation. That light that lives within usis from a higher source of power. In this higher source, we can trust its validation and peace. Ultimately, allowing a maintenance of stable emotions.

In my first marriage, I can remember how perfect the relationship seemed to be. Everything was amazing in the beginning. The relationship was fresh, it was new, everyone was happy, and many people admired some of the early accomplishments that was attained. Once expectations started to change the environment and tone of the relationship changed. We were no longer happy, and the smallest things turned into arguments. The relationship became toxic. Family members had opinions about how things should have been operating and there were tons of bickering and gossiping to go around for days.

This was an immediate threat to the idea of life that I wanted to create for myself. As long as I was going along and meeting the expectations of others, there were no problems. As soon as I stepped outside of that mold of ideas, you could feel the tension every time I walked into a room. The love turned to hate and resentment very quickly.

When my second ex-wife left me, a new realm of possibilities opened up. New relationships, new opportunities, fresh ideas of who I was and who I've been and who I am becoming was confirmed. I was so intense and adamant of my ideas I had to pursue them.

Unfavorable circumstances are almost always inevitable when you're not clear about the intention and expectations of each relationship. People in your life should have a purpose and they should have an idea of your expectations of them. Don'tallow yourself to continue down a dead-end road with an unproductive relationship because you will always find yourself trapped fighting for the ideas that you really believe in.

Coming to grips with this is painful. For me, it led to two divorces. However, the freedom that I have gained to be the best version of myself is totally liberating. Each marriage revealed valuable lessons about who I was as a person and who I needed to be. I had to detach my emotions from the truth of being divorced twice to even finish this book. At a few points, I felt like a complete failure, but I had to dig deep within to pick up the pieces of my life to continue moving forward.

No one wakes up in the morning and seeks to be toxic in relationships. We'reall searching to fulfill needs within us where voids may have been created during our upbringing. Each of us were born into different environments, with different values, and different cultures. It is okay to have differences. It is not okay to crucify an individual because of those differences.

Doing so will cause any relationship to turn toxic regardless of any positive intention. Healthy relationships are comprised of two individuals that respect the other's perspective, values, and ideas.

Photo Credit: thejenmoff.com

This chart not only represent essential and effective characteristic traits of a healthy relationship, but it also demonstrates mannerisms that each individual should have with themselves. We miss the mark when we enter into a relationship and expect our friend, spouse, or partner to give us something we don't even practice. How could we expect someone else to be accountable for their actions or behaviors when we won't take accountability for our own? Are you honest with yourself? Can you admit when you are wrong? Healthy relationships begin with you.

Being accountable for your behaviors, decisions, choices, and habits are vital if you desire to have a healthy relationship. Becoming *whole* is work you must completewithin-intentionally. Trusting your intuition and peaceful effective communication are all qualities that must be practiced. Intentional personal reflection to assist in becoming more aware.

Being aware in moments of discomfort is key to being sure that you can survive toxic situations. Understanding how to handle a disagreement or agreeing to disagree without holding grudges is crucial. Another important factor to consider is knowing the type of energy you bring to thesituation.

Life has many ways of bringing you to a humble state. I have to laugh as I type this because there are times when I take myself a bit too serious. The ultimate message of this chapter is to understand that the only way out is to go through tough moments with positive reinforcements. It's the simplest statement but the hardest to do especially when another human life is involved in the equation.

What happens in your relationship when you no longer have the job you had in the beginning of the relationship? What happens in a relationship when you quit your job? What happens when you have had five jobs in five years because each year another job offered you more money? What happens when you don't agree with an idea? Is the other individual upset because your theory maybe different? Small issues can cause a relationship to become toxic.

There is no one to blame for failed relationships or friendships. There are only lessons to be learned. The key is being aware of the emotions that you're feeling when certain things happen. Having a mutual veneration for individuals is essential and at the core of healthy relationships.

Unhealthy relationships come with different toxins. More than half of society is dealing with baggage and past issues that are always exposed. If you are dealing with past issues, find a way to release them from your mind, your thoughts, and your heart. Don't internalize hurt or pain, because it comes out in one way or another. You control your life with your thoughts. Many people self-loathe but doing so is such a waste of time. The only person you have control over is yourself. You can change how you see a situation or remove yourself from the situation all together.

Stop resenting others or what happened to you. Resentment is reliving the pain and hurt over and over again. The only antidote to resentment is forgiveness. You never have to forget, but you must forgive to move forward.

Sleep walking through life like the characters in the *Walking Dead* is not an option. Life is about waking up and whatever it takes to wake you up to no longer hold on to grudges, no longer be resentful, to move out of the past, to step out of history, you must take the necessarysteps.

Moving forward is a process. It takes courage to confront the things in your heart that continue to make you feel a certain way and not happy or content. Step out of whatever happened to you and start to live right now. Be aware of what IS happening to you and what you CAN do something about. Decide what you control, decide whatever that takes, then that's what is necessary to move youforward.

Poison comes in many forms...and the things that are screaming to you are loud and clear. The media has the ability to influence a mass amount of people. But most of the information that is being reported is senseless, bias, opinionated, and untrue.

POISON-Toxins.

This is our society's cancer and one of the reasons why divorce is at an all-time high. The media's depiction of what a relationship should *look* like or how it should be managed based on others experience causes epic failure. Movies, TV shows, talk shows all create an illusion of how relationships should work when respect and honest communication is the central efficient way to be involved in a relationship.

Communication

Building a strong foundation of communication in relationships is more critical than you may think. Clarity of purpose and intention can save a lot of wasted time, heartache, families hating each other, and potentially children growing up without both parents. We have a great understanding of the English language; however, we often fail to communicate efficiently and effectively.

Fifteen years ago, when I met the in-laws of my first marriage, I was really impressed. They were a close-knit group. Very loving, caring and we shared a lot of moments of laughter. During one of the first conversations with one of the key influencers in the family, a very important question came up, "What are your intentions with our baby?"

My response was simple, I plan to marry her and have a successful military career. I did not go into the details of what that meant. I did not communicate that I was not going to spend twenty years in the military. My intent was not to mislead the family in any way. The communication was not as clear as it could have been (looking back).

When I made the decision to join a financial planning firm there were arguments that referenced our first conversation about my intentions. I couldn't understand why anyone was against me making thiscareer transition. Becoming an investment advisor and being registered with the SEC was an accomplishment because I completed this goal without having my bachelor's degree. Having achieved a portion of my dream without realizing it was not exciting because I had to deal with the arguments of me making a careertransition.

My vision of what I wanted to do with my life began to exceed the initial vision I had when joining the Marine Corps. The change was mental, in which, something that wasn't able tobe seen visibly. The fault in this situation was with my inability to communicate this change. Epiphanies happen often in our lives and many times we don't communicate these changes.

It's no different than when you hang out with a group of your friends that you haven't seen in a while. You may hear something like, "You've changed." A lot of times this change is not physical. The change is mental. You show up looking like the same person you were five years ago without any physical evidence of your new mindset.

These changes are critical in relationships. Outside of substance abuse or infidelity, finances and the lack of proper communication is the number one cause for couples to become divorced. Shana Lebowitz, writer for Business Insider, completed a list of common reasons why some relationships just don't make it. Researchers interviewed couples to determine the why.

One couple simply stated that, "We'd have an argument over something really simple and it would turn into just huge, huge fights." Lebowitz added, "there's no guarantee that any conflict-management strategy can prevent divorce. But for couples who feel as if they're always having the same fight, researchers recommend simply listening and displaying empathy. Instead of always cutting your partner off so you can share your side of the story, try hearing the person out and reflecting back what he or she has told you."

"Financial problems are another common reason for divorce. One person in the 2013 study said: "I had a severe illness for almost a year, and I was the only employed person [before that] so obviously money ran very short."

Interestingly, couples therapists say money is one of the main reasons people seek marriage counseling. (Problems with parenting and physical intimacy are two others.)

That's why Business Insider's Lauren Lyons Cole, a certified financial planner, recommends that couples know everything about each other's money before they get married — from their student-loan debt to their spending habits."

Divorce is not just the end of a marriage. It's the end of momentum. Momentum in finances, momentum spiritually, come through divorces. I have found myself financially depleted several times. It leaves me wondering about my desire to build an enterprise while pursuing an intimate relationship. Is it even possible?

The desire for me to build will always be a part of me. It has always been a part of me. When I left Greensboro, AL I had a plan to build a life that I didn't have growing up. I was able to accomplish that. Soon after accomplishing that task, my mind immediately shifted to the next idea of starting my own business.

Entrepreneurship is not for the faint of heart. The journey will break you down. It will have you looking crazy because you're chasing a vision in your mind that only you can see. You'll have many nights that you lose sleep. Unfortunately for me, it has cost me two marriages, lost time, and not living in the same house as my children.

Andrew Thomas (2017) wrote an article about the truths of dating entrepreneurs on inc.com that was very interesting. He talked about how these types of people are exciting. The difficulty with these people that arise, is when they try to build an intimate relationship. His list includes last-minute changes, the relationship being an emotional roller coaster, the non-entrepreneur would be competing for attention, long work hours, constant interruptions, constant travel, working on the weekends, and their business is yourbusiness.

Although life is an individual journey of self-discovery, self-control should be the conclusion to the epidemic of failed relationships. We are displaced from this idea because of programming. Poison and toxins that drown out *that* voice is reasoning. It confuses you. As soon as you begin to feel confused, that is a sign that it is not the *real you. i*t's not the *something* that effortlessly guides you. That *something told me to or not to* is your compass. It is your invisible satellite. Your internal GPS that guides you. It is also betting on you in all instances. It is your blueprint. Not the ideologies of other people.

My intimate relationships ended with mixed tones. Neither party wanted the relationships to end, but the tools to sustain them had not yet been discovered. Several counseling sessions took place to attain these tools, but they didn't happen until the relationships were over. Mosttimes, the only way out is *through.*

Take a close look at your circle or all of the relationships that you are involved with. Any person that has a way of eating away at your belief system and self-esteem is toxic. If you have lost your sense of identity and your personal priorities are not priority to you, you are in a manipulative relationship. Manipulators are skillful at getting what they want.

Let's take a look at the friendships where there is an extreme sense of self-importance. Narcissistic individuals are solely focused on their needs leaving you feeling disappointed and unfulfilled. For instance, what about the pessimistic family member that can never appreciate the positive in life. If you speak about how beautiful the weather is, they will tell you the forecast calls for rain in five days. *Downers* are similar to dream killers and take the joy out of everything. Never take on the mindset of someone who is consumed withnegativity.

Tell me you are conscious of the relationship with your girlfriend who judges your make-up, your style, your smile in pictures, and your relationship with your other friends. This individual is self-righteous and believes that their thought process is right because of their truths. Examine your relationships with this person. No one has the right to judge anything. We all have vices that we will probably have to work on until the day we die. It isinexorable.

What about the spouse who tells you, "you can't do it" every time you have an idea. Or as soon as you attempt to accomplish a lofty goal, you are pulled down by their fear of not wanting to take on such a challenge. Anyone that tells you something is impossible is a dream killer. Dream killers had to have itsown chapter because of the intensity of that subject and those type of people. Progress and change can only occur from doing new things and innovating. You have to dream of the impossible and know there are no physicallimitations.

Get rid of the *Insincere Isabellas* as well. Have you ever experienced someone who is not genuine and build relationships on superficial criteria? The shallow people that only date certain types of people because of status or class. Another example, when you are in need of a friend, constructive criticism, or support, they would rather see you fail or make a fool of yourself....TOXIC RELATIONSHIP.

Think about the people that you spend time trying to please but end up losing yourself in the process. Have you ever been in a relationship where all of your time, resources, and energy is required but all you feel is worn out and your needs have been sacrificed? This person has taken you for granted and no matter what you have contributed you can never give enough to make them happy.

Who is the person in your life that takes you for granted, have unrealistic expectations of you, or they continuously fault you and never take responsibility? Whose fault is it when we are knee deep in a relationship with *Never Enough Ned?*

Manipulative Marcy, Narcissistic Nia, Debbie Downer, Judgmental Jeff, Dream Killer Dave, Insecure/Insincere Isabella, and *Never Enough Ned* have nothing on *Disrespectful Raymond.* This type of individual will say or do inappropriate things that will rock your core. A person that uses your secrets against you or states slandering demeaning things about you have no sense of boundaries and do not respect you or your feelings. Can you personally place aname by each of these examples?

Learning how to segment individuals in your life helps to eliminate toxic relationships from the beginning. Energy does not lie. That feeling that you get when you are in certain people's presence is real and you should begin to use that as your discernment. Anyone that confuses your emotional stability are either not good for you, or effective communication must be explored in that relationship.

Understanding that you will only have a few Confidants, but many constituents and comrades will help you determine if combining your energy with theirs will be mutually beneficial. The concluding goal is to build relationships with those that add and multiply to not only you-but you to them.

Spiritual Growth has three elements/components:

-Relationships (Your interaction and behavior with others)
-Truth (Honesty)
-Time (Patience/Humility)

Relationships are critical to life. We are always in a relationship with people around us. We have free will to make choices about who we decide to enter into relationships with. We have that freedom. It is wise to know that we cannot be in relationships with everybody. Our choices come in a variety of things. Who we choose to enter into a relationship with, whether it is an intimate relationship, a friendship, or a partnership; it is still based on choice.

Four of the ten commandments deal with our relationship to God while the other six deal with our relationships with people. All ten are about relationships and how you treat other people, not your wealth or accomplishment and this is the most enduring impact you can leave on earth. Real maturity (and growth) is demonstrated in relationships.

Many people grow up in families with unhealthy relationships, so they lack the relational skills needed for healthy authentic relationships (whether it's business or personal). This is why truth and honesty are so important. In any relationship, you can trust a person that communicates to you their concerns. We as a people being connected through One source must care enough to lovingly speak the truth, even when you would prefer to *fluff*, sugar coat, or even ignore an issue. Most don't have people in their life who love them enough to tell them the truth (even when it's painful), so they continue in self-destructive ways. *An honest answer is a sign of true friendships,* Ephesians 4:15.

Many relationships are destroyed by a lack of Honesty. Real relationships (i.e. marriage, partnership, friendship) are developed through being authentic or frank. There is a big difference in *being real* and being authentic. *Being real* is not a license to say anything you want wherever and whenever you want. There is always a right time and right way to do everything. Thoughtless, careless words and actions leave lastingwounds. *Even a fool is considered wise when he doesn't speak his whole mind.* (Proverb)

Chapter Four

Mindset

Developing your mindset to become independent and living the life of your dreams takes a while for most. There are mental challenges we all have to fight or conquer, and it has to do with how we are socialized within society.

Socialization causes us to think a certain way based on the status quo. If everybody is doing something, then it must be right? Wrong! We have a society of people today that never question most of the things that they've been taught.

Earning a living by working forty hours a week and making about $20 an hour is the "norm" in our society.

Socialization tells you to go to college, get a nine to five, invest in your 401k, make sure you have credit cards for emergencies, get married, purchase a house, be fruitful and multiply, and then train your children to do the same damn thing. Now we are in a trap. No one is telling us to focus on building our own micro-enterprise. Which is simply a different conversation.

We should attend school to educate ourselves about an industry that we are interested in learning more about. Making a living with our natural strengths should be programmed into our mindset. Or we should be taught to start a business utilizing our abilities and skills. From that business, we should be trained to use our profits and assets as leverage to increase our net worth.

We are not taught how to build net worth in our education system. Our economic system functions with debt. Debt seems to be our modern-day slavery. We spend all of our lives on that tread mill of accumulation. We know we are on this tread mill and we convince ourselves that we like what we do. We wake up every morning miserable and dread to hear the alarm clock ring in the morning.

Have you ever felt this way? Are you feeling this way right now? As a human, we all have a deep burning desire to explore and dream. When talking to most individuals this desire is usually different than what we find ourselves doing on a daily basis. How do we sustain ourselves to eventually do the things that we love to do?

We have to develop the mindset to handle the flow of small amounts of money before we're able to handle large sums of money. I had the ability to make money but not the mindset to handle it. I was not taught the importance of financial literacy. My mentors helped me with producing the income, but I had no clue how to manage that income or how to make sure it grew. In 2009, I decided to transition from being a solider. I was questioned as to why I was ending my career with the military because the perception was there were no jobs. The economy recently was recovering from the major recession hit of 2008.

Everyone pushed their ideas off on me. The military was comfortable and provided a steady income, however, that was their idea of what I should have been doing with my life; including my first ex-wife. Others will gladly push their ideas of how you should live your life. We must learn to stand as the defender of our ideas and as an individual. My mindset had changed regarding what I wanted for my life, once again.

I'm pretty sure you've heard people say, "If I had a million dollars, I would do this. If I had a fifty thousand dollars, I would do that." More than likely they haven't acquired that amount of money because their mindset has not allowed it to happen. You cannot make more than what your mind will allow you to make. There are many people who believe they are high-minded thinkers. *High-minded thinkers* believe they possess an elevated level of thinking when in fact they are just ignorant. The amount of currency you possess determines what level your mindset is financially. In a capitalistic society, that's how we measure finances.

You have to accept the level where you are in order to move to the next level. Gratitude plays a major part in attracting more into your life. As Americans we should not be complacent and should always work with a sense of urgency. The resources that we need to earn more, learn more, or be more are right at our fingertips.

Having faith and believing that we all have the ability to produce the outcome we desire is important to creating the ultimate dream life. Believing that achieving your dreams are even possible even when everything around you is saying that it is not, is the resilience needed to live that dream life. Be willing to continue moving forward, although, you may not feel like it. Doing things when you don't feel like doing them is the mindset needed to develop your goals and bring your dreams into reality.

Being born in America provides tons of resources that other countries wish they had. This also gives us a great opportunity to produce and create realities that may not exist in other parts of the world.

Our children have access to possibilities (tangible and intangible) that other children do not have in other countries. Verses teaching or programming our kids how to be or become consumers, we should instead teach them how to generate an income in high school with the things they love. Instead of buying Nike sneakers, they should buy Nike's stock.

I remember being in Chicago showing my kids how to trade and I made $1000 in about thirty minutes. I was showing them how to trade stocks with a computer and an internet connection. I hope that moment inspired them how to think beyond a cubicle. I don't want them to settle for a job. I want them to see how they can generate money from a computer and an internet connection.

As Americans, I don't think we fully understand money because we are not taught how to make money work for us. We are taught how to work for money. Once we receive that paycheck, we are taught to go out and spend it at the malls or anywhere else that has a sale. The systematic way of living is not only modern-day slavery for most, but it keeps individuals in debt and in bondage for most of their life. I can't speak for many, but I can use myself as a primeexample.

Serving in two branches of the military taught me the value of being in control of my time. In the military, you are told when to wake up, when to eat, how much you should weigh, and everyone wore the same uniform. I loved the structure; however, I longed to be in an environment where I could express myself though independence of thoughts and ideas.

I have also enjoyed times recently where I was able to generate income without dealing with many people. Utilizing the stock market can help create freedom. You can make money from the comforts of your home and some days it takes less than thirty minutes to make a few thousand dollars. These are ideas to help jump start the engine in your brain about things you could do to earn extra income for yourself. Please take the levels of risk into consideration before jumping into anything.

Here's the route several people that I know have taken. They went to a four-year university for their Bachelor's degree, a two-year online university for their Masters, and then another year to receive a second Masters. Once their adult life starts, they have already started it in a huge amount of debt due to student loans.

The idea to live the so-called "American Dream" starts to kick in and they purchase a home. Living the American dream, adds more debt to an already growing pile of bills. Throw a few credit cards into this mix, and we all know how the story ends. Can we say maxed out?

With a salary, credit card bills and student loans, we can see how it would be hard for anyone to get out of debt, and it leads most families sinking further and further in sinking sand. They become unhappy because of the situation and the mind gets cloudy with the issues of life. They forget all about their creative powers that they possess because they become consumed with working daily just to pay the bills. Most people don't envision the entrapment for their lives. They begin to search for a way out of the indebted lifestyle. The system has created another depressed customer that drug companies can sell their products too.

What is the "systematic way of living?" It is typically for the average American; being born; going to elementary, middle and high school with no worries; being sent off to college for about four to seven years; finally getting into the workforce with worries of being successful, advancements, and debts, getting married; purchasing a home; raising a family; and working for about 30-40 years until retirement. The cycle is continuous and helps the economy with cash flow and jobs.

Consider this idea for a moment. In order for the world to spin on its axis and no one fall off with how fast it's spinning, there must be a perfect formula that takes strategic execution. With six quadrillion kilograms (estimated) hanging on a string (figuratively speaking) many are baffled at this scientific wander.

Although this is not a science lesson there is a science into understanding what makes the world "go 'round." What else makes the world "go 'round?" Is it when people work their careersand jobs every day to ensure that products and services are provided and/or sold. The economy or the universe has been built on supply and demand. Consumers or clients will purchase what you have if they need or want it. In acknowledging that, there must be people to work in every industry imaginable or created. You would also think that everyone isn't called to be an Entrepreneur... but we all are, and I have a philosophy for you to consider.

Everyone is an Entrepreneur

We are programmed to believe that we go to college, get a job, make a family, buy a home and live happily ever after. What we are not told is that college degrees are just as expensive as a Benz, Beemer, or any luxury care. To take that a step further, didn't you go to college to better yourself? Didn't you go so you could afford a GREAT paying job - to purchase the best (i.e. Benz, Beemers) or anything you want? In the last three years, there weren't many jobs for new graduates or former employees to choose from and that alone should get your souls stirred up about Entrepreneurship!

I don't have anything against investing in education but at the age of 25, the average American is in debt just from student loans. Starting out $20,000-$60,000 in the hole is a bit backwards and is definitely not how you should start. Something is *very* wrong with this picture. Our lives shouldn't be this way and in leading this new generation, I am telling you to create your own destiny. Make your own path. There are many self-taught entrepreneurs. The library has free books. The Internet has information to infinity. Anything worth having requires an investment. But, my friend, the investment doesn't have to always be money. Time is the best thing you can invest when trying to achieve anything. Taking the time to understand, research, plan, coordinate, organize, and execute is essential in understanding the Entrepreneurial journey.

I know we all are blessed with something that we can do really well without the help of education or practice makes most of us a micro-enterprise. If this world is set up on the concept of supply and demand, then why aren't jobs hiring sub-contractors? Just by hiring a sub-contractor takes away so many expenses such as health insurance, electricity, and I can go on. If I am good at what I do, why can't I be sub-contracted to provide your business what is required to operate it? (Oh and not below what I am worth!) There's a market for your skillset. It takes time and effort to carve out theniche.

I don't believe that the world was created for there to be "masters and slaves--managers and employees." The simple concept of supply and demand has turned into people having to commit to making a living based on someone else's terms. If I have something you want, you pay me for it. It should be that simple. Of course, I don't know how this concept turned into you working for me or me working for you. We are supposed to work together. "We", meaning you and I, and anyone else who has a product or service that I may need to operate my business. The economy being without jobs, should prompt individuals to go ahead and take the risk of starting their own.

Again, the military trained me to lead and help those who were not able to help themselves. We all have different skill sets that we perform at various levels of mastery. If you are able to withstand the criticism of being an individual, you will be on your way to creating the lifestyle that you desire. I don't ride on a white horse giving demands or orders. We work together to empower and assist other people to become the best and give the best. That's what excellence is!

So now your question may be, well what about the slackers? You replace them with other sub-contractors who will do the job well or better. Just like there is a variety of everything in the world, there is a variety of people who offer the same services/gifts/talents that you need to accomplish your goal, and they may be really good at what they do. Society is set up for those who are most fit. There are the ones who survive. Being independent requires mental toughness.

Summary

Big businesses were once medium businesses and medium businesses were once small businesses and that small business started with one person: An Entrepreneur.

People, the time is now to get out there and make your dreams a reality. You can survive. No matter what it looks like to others. Figure out what you love to do. What is your passion? What is it that you would do even if you weren't paid what you wanted to be paid but you could still find fulfillment doing? What gives you an adrenaline rush? What can you do better than most without schooling, training, or practice? Do you know a market that is untapped that you can tap into and really become successful?

There is a story about a wealthy man who had three servants. The wealthy man went away for a long period of time, but he gave one servant a huge amount of money, another servant just enough money, and the last servant only a small portion of what was his.

He provided the amount of money to each based on their abilities. He told these three servants to invest this money while he was away. The story goes on to say that the two servants that received the most money invested the money and had received twice the amount that was given to them. But the last servant buried the money, didn't touch it, and didn't invest it.

He was afraid to take risks. He was complacent and pessimistic about what could possibly happen. Well the wealthy man returns to his servants and was expecting great news from the three servants but was really anxious to see what the servants did to increase the money that he providedthem.

When he saw that his first two servants not only made more money than he anticipated, but made a huge profit, he allowed them to enjoy with him the increase. The third servant thought that he did the right thing by just holding on to what was given to him and was excited to be able to give back the money.

The wealthy man could not believe that the servant wasted time, did not make a profit, and was disappointed that the servant did not have enough sense to put the money in a bank to just gain interest.

The servant did not invest or put the money to use, the wealthy man took the money back from him, gave it to the servant who he gave the most money to, and explained to him the importance of utilizing your gifts, talents, and resources to advance in life.

He also fired him and wanted nothing to do with him because he felt that the servant was lazy. The third servant began with nothing and because of his lack of hopefulness, he ended up with nothing.

Are you operating like the third servant? Are you holding on to everything that you get instead of investing it into something that is going to make a better life for yourself or someone else? Are you ambiguous? Are you refusing to be a risk taker? Are you afraid of the "what ifs?"

As I write this section of the book, I can honestly say to you that I have felt all of the emotions that you may have felt when I read those questions I just asked. At times, I have even thought that maybe I am a bit crazy for having this deep, down, and burning desire to be an independent business owner. Why can't I not just shut this desire off, and maintain a regular job like the most of society?

I have no answer for that last question. My quest continues on this journey. It is not easy. It is extremely hard. There are times when I have enormous amounts of stress. Times when I am not able to see the light at the end of the tunnel. Times when people have quit on me because of their fears of limitation and lack. Maybe you have even wanted to quit reading this book because you don't see how this story relates to your life.

The only way out of uncomfortable circumstances is resilience. Will you quit when things get tough? Will you give in when most people are in disagreement with your ideology? You can't quit. You must continue. You must live your dream life and you must start building that life today.

Chapter Five

Living the Life of Your Dreams

Imagine living the life of your dreams and the first thing that comes to mind is having a million dollars in the bank, being a millionaire, driving fancy cars, and maybe even living in a huge house. All of these things are nice. I even have my own ambition to do many of the items that are mentioned above. However, living your dream life is simple than many of us think. It does not require lavish luxuries and excessive material possessions.

The beautiful part about living the life of your dreams is thatit is totally up to you to define what that means for yourself. No marketing promo can tempt you into living a life that you don't decide to live for yourself. No flashy rap video can force you into buying things that you can't afford. This decision is yours to make and yours alone.

In 2005, I served the last year of my military duties with the Marine Corps. I was serving as an associate minister at the church that I was attending in Norfolk, VA. There was an opportunity for a group of people to go on a mission trip to Ethiopia. I took all of the money that I had saved in my thrift savings plan to take the trip. This trip totally changed my life.

One of the first experiences of this trip happened while sitting on Ethiopian Airline in Washington, D.C. I'm sitting there excited about this part of the trip because we were actually about to leave the states and head for Africa. "Wow! I'm heading to Africa" was a statement that I repeated several times in my mind.

As we were waiting to leave, the lady sitting next to me starts to speak to me in the ancient language, Amharic. This is the language that is spoken in Ethiopia. I didn't realize it at the moment; however, as I reflected on this moment over the years, I realized that she acknowledged my Ethiopian roots. I like to tell people that my roots trace back to Ethiopia. After all, it is the place where the oldest human fossils were discovered.

Anytime I see an Ethiopian in America, I try to stop and speak with them briefly. Connecting with my African culture makes me feel proud. I can actually say that I had the privilege of visiting the motherland, the land of my descendants. This opportunity has changed my perspective on life in America. The things that we were taught growing up were once again challenged in my mind.

How could a continent of people exist in a world surrounded by wealthy nations, and many countries on the continent suffer from extreme poverty? The answer to this question is a totally different discussion. Let's save that for another book.

I was twenty-two years old when I experienced this trip. This is an experience that many African Americans don't get the chance to take, or don't seek out as an opportunity. It left me asking even more questions. Why do African American go to places like Mexico, Paris, Italy, etc. yet never take the journey back to Africa?

The experience was so rich. We sat with ambassadors discussing many of the issues that some of the villages were experiencing. We took a trip to a hospital where young girls from the country were suffering from complications of having a child too soon. Many of the men in their villages were infected with HIV. Their beliefs were if they had sex with a virgin, they would rid themselves of the disease. What a horrible experience for the girls. Something like this actually takes place in this world.

I realized that being born in America is actually the dream of many across the world. Other people from different nations fight hard to get to this country. To have a chance to live the life that is not afforded to them being born outside of this country. Even the ghettos in America has no comparison to the ghettos in Shanty Town,Ethiopia.

This also led me to another question. Why are most Americans unappreciative of the miracle of being born in this country? Yes! Being born in America is a miracle. There are so many things afforded to us in this country that other countries can't even imagine. Many times, most of us can't see beyond the city that we were raised. We never venture out to see the world. Therefore, our perspectives can only be as broad as our experiences in life. We have a limited view of the world, yet we try to generalize the way the world actually operates.

For example, I grew up in Greensboro, AL. Greensboro is a very small rural town. The closest town is Tuscaloosa, AL. which is twenty-two miles north. If you drove down Main St., at the end you'll find a large slave plantation called Magnolia Grove. There are many negative connotations about slave plantations and being African American. We drove by this plantation every day on our way to school. I could have easily grew up with a negative taste in my mouth regarding Caucasians. But I didn't because some of the most influential people in my childhood were white.

When I was twelve years old, I got into trouble with law enforcement. I was having fun with my cousin and we ended up shooting a window out of a potato chip truck as he passed by our house on his daily routine. Look at what a silly joke could have caused an injury to a man to lose his job.

The Sheriff, who was a white man, refused to take us to the juvenile detention center. For some reason, the only thing that I could think of was failing the grade and repeating the next year. It was a miracle that he didn't take us to jail. My life would have been ruined and this is usually what happens to most young men in environments like the one I grew up in. I will never forget that day.

Another influence was my baseball coach. He would pick me up for our baseball games and even make sure I had something to eat afterwards. I loved riding with him because I knew after the game, I would get a chance to get a hefty meal.

These influences changed the perspective I had growing up in this small town. When I joined the military, I was ready to face people from different cultures which shifted my perspective once again. No matter which culture we're from, most of us are facing many of the same problems. We all want our families to be happy, safe, and we want them to have some of the luxuries in life. I was experiencing life beyond what I could even imagine growing up. I was living life beyond what I dreamed.

At the time I was not aware of this, I was constantly pushing for more. Being unsatisfied with any accomplishments, I kept pursuing and being the best at what I was doing. I was obsessed with success. I drove myself to the limits. I have a hard time even this day relaxing to enjoy some of the fruits of my labor. Until one day I had an epiphany.

I was on the golf course on a Saturday morning and I could hear the birds chirping although it was cloudy. A storm was rolling in and I realized that I had accomplished everything I wanted to accomplish in life, except having a million dollars in the bank. I also realized that I was living a pretty good life without this money in the bank. The only thing that the money would have changed for me was doing more of what I was already doing. I would travel more, play more golf, and enjoy spending time with my family. I was living the life of my dreams. I had escaped the strong holds that held me impoverished or what society considers poverty in America.

Your dream life can only be defined by you. Most of the time we are bombarded with ads, commercials, rap videos, and many other things that entice us to want more than we already have. It creates the appetite within you that somehow you are not enough. You need more. If you're not careful, you'll find yourself chasing these items. These items are expensive. I'm not only talking about the money that it takes to acquire these items. I'm talking about the emotional, physical, and psychological strain it takes to achieve and sustain high levels of success.

The family of high producers may have enough money to go around. However, the time spent away from the family to produce the income is a cost that the family has to pay. What happens if Dad is always on the road because of the demands of his job? What happens if Mommy is always on callbecause she's a doctor and she must go to the hospital for an emergency?

Rebecca Rosen described this in an article in 2015, that two income families feel like they are always rushed. Most of the time, there's not enough time in the day to spend with the family. However, the financial trade-offs that come with two-income families are not without cost. That cost is passed on to the family. Families are found being cash rich and time poor. Is this the idea of your dream life?

Living in a capitalistic society, we are in constant pursuit of more capital. We make it. We spend it. Then back to making more. The cycle never ends. There's rarely a time when we step back to take a look at the dream of being born in this country. We live in America. Everyone can be considered rich if the perspective is viewed from someone in a third world country. We're rich in resources. Yet, it is our constant drive to have more, mixed with the marketing machine that wants us to spend more, that drives us down a trial of over consumption. We end up spending resources that could help build our dream lives. By the time we're forty, the realization sets in about how much time we've wasted.

Due to this fact, I have conducted a simple overview of the things I had accomplished in my life. I compared these accomplishments to the things that I wanted growing up as a child. I suggest you do the same with your life. Let me know how it goes once you've done this. Here's a simple version of my analysis. I hope that it helps you to simplify your life.

I mentioned earlier in the book that I grew up poor. This reality drove me to make sure that my living conditions as an adult were different than my living conditions as a child. I was able to build my first house at twenty and purchase my second house at thirty-four. Those two accomplishments satisfied my idea of the living conditions that I dreamt about. Check off from my list of goals.

I have traveled to Mexico twice, Africa, Iraq, Germany, Trinidad and Tobago, and too many other states within America. I could only imagine going to some of these places as a child. My outlook on the world has been broadened because of those experiences. I had a check book when I was in high school with the globe as the backdrop on the checks. I wanted to travel. Check off from my list of goals.

I have three amazingly talented children; Camille, Sydney, and AJ. Although I am not the perfect Father, they are the perfect children. They're smart, witty, talented, and confident in who they are as individuals. My goal is to live out the rest of my days making sure that I am able to pass to them an inheritance and legacy. The good book says that a wise man leaves an inheritance for his children's children. That is my life's mission. I'm simply hustling for my last name. Check off from my list of goals.

I have been married and divorced twice. I was not the perfect husband, but love is perfect. I have learned that it is very hard for human beings to produce the highest ideas of what love really is or what love really means. However, I am not bitter. I carry the lessons that I've found out about myself as a man. I strive to become a better man as I move forward into the future. As I complete this paragraph, I am waiting for my divorce settlement to be agreed upon. Divorce number two is right around the corner. I am still excited about the rest of my life. Check.

I have faced many challenges in my life. Those challenges are what makes the dream so sweet. The key ingredients to living the life of your dreams requires consistency, relentlessness, resilience, and faith. Being able to talk about your losses, take responsibilities for those losses, and to pick yourself up off of the floor is what life's journey is all about.

I have faith that things will be better than they are right now. You must maintain faith in better days if your current situation is not ideal. Know that the not so ideal days are also a part of your dream. Life is not hocus pocus; it's not abra kadabra (I'm not sure if I spelled that right, but hey). You will have to go through tough times. You will have to find a way to keep going even when you feel like quitting. Don't ever quit.

As long as you're in the fight, you have a chance. As soon as you decide to quit, you quit on millions of people who are counting on your gift. There is some man, woman, boy, or girl who's counting on you to speak life from your point-of-view. You're unique. You have to believe it.

You have to believe that you're already living the life of your dreams right now. Yes, there may be some things that you desire, you're living the dream right now. Hold that thought in your imagination. Envision yourself moving towards your next goal. The next person that you meet could be the key to opening a door that you couldn't open foryourself.

The universe is waiting for you to have faith; then work. Because we have all heard the statement that "faith without works is dead." Don't have dead faith! Have faith that works through life's circumstances! You have to have grit!

It's The Only Way Out!

It is how I escaped poverty and I'm living the life of my dreams. I'm experiencing the best that life has to offer. You can too!

Notes

1. Philip Perry. Big Think Smarter Faster: How to test your emotional intelligence and use it to improve your life – Retrieved 2.16.18

2. Thomas, Andrew. Inc.com- Retrieved 12.15.2017_ www.inc.com/andrew-thomas/10-brutal-truths-about-dating-an-entrepreneur.html

3. Prof Michael Munger, Duke, 2012
   Should Majorities Decide Everything?
   Retrieved 03.11.18

4. Rebecca Rosen. The Atlantic. 11.04.2015_ https://www.theatlantic.com/business/archive/2015/11/work-life-balance-pew-report/414028/
   Retrieved 03.11.18

5. Levine, M. (2006). The price of privilege: How parental pressure and material advantage are creating a generation of disconnected and unhappy kids. New York, NY, US: HarperCollins Publishers.

6. Katie Little, May 25, 2016, article CNBC.com
   10 traits rich people have in common
   Retrieved 03.11.18

7. Shana Lebowitz-12.18.17. Business Insider:
   7 Common Reasons People say they got divorce_ http://www.businessinsider.com/why-people-get-divorced-2017-12#financial-problems-6
   Retrieved 03.07.18

8. Medicallyreviewed by George T. Krucik, MD, MBA on January 28, 2015 — Written by Ann Pietrangelo. Healthline: Depression and Mental Health by the Numbers: Facts, Statistics, and You_
https://www.healthline.com/health/depression/facts-statistics-infographic#modal-close
Retrieved 03.26.18

9. Rupert Neate. 11.14.17 The Guardian: Richest 1% own half the world's wealth, study finds_
https://www.theguardian.com/inequality/2017/nov/14/worlds-richest-wealth-credit-suisse
Retrieved 03.26.18

10. Aimee Picchi. 11.14.17: CBS.com: Money Watch: World's Richest 1% control more than half of all wealth
https://www.cbsnews.com/news/richest-1-percent-control-more-than-half-of-all-wealth/
Retrieved 03.26.18

11. Rick Warren's Purpose Driven Life

www.ingramcontent.com/pod-product-compliance
Ingram Content Group UK Ltd.
Pitfield, Milton Keynes, MK11 3LW, UK
UKHW020135250726
13967UKWH00002B/672